THE BOY ON FAIRFIELD STREET

How Ted Geisel Grew Up to Become Dr. Seuss

By Kathleen Krull

Paintings by Steve Johnson and Lou Fancher

With decorative illustrations by Dr. Seuss

Random House 🏠 New York

Once upon a time, there lived a boy who feasted on books and was wild about animals.

He was born in 1904 and lived in the best of all possible places—74 Fairfield Street in Springfield, Massachusetts. The gray three-story house was exactly three blocks from the public library. And it was just six blocks from the zoo.

This boy loved lots of things besides reading and animals—sledding, doodling, trying on costumes, singing around the piano with his family, exploring the green fields of nearby Forest Park. All in all, he excelled at fooling around.

No one on Fairfield Street could have said how Ted Geisel, that funny boy, would turn out.

No one in the world could have.

Especially Ted.

At dinner, Ted's family gathered around the huge oak table. Often they talked about the animals in the zoo.

Ted's father, Theodor Geisel, worked in the family business. But he also helped out at the zoo and eventually was superintendent of parks—which meant he actually *ran* the zoo. Ted would eat baked beans and bratwurst and thrill to stories of stubborn bears and chattering monkeys, prowling lions and wild wolves.

At night, their hoots and cries sometimes found their way into his dreams.

Ted's mother, Henrietta Seuss Geisel, helped him find books at the library. Her dream was to get Ted and his sister, Marnie, into college, as the first in their family to go. Perhaps Ted might even grow up to become "Dr. Geisel."

Each night she lulled them to sleep with stories and nonsense verse, like the names of pies: "Apple, mince, lemon . . . peach, apricot, pineapple . . . blueberry, coconut, custard, and SQUASH!"

Ted would listen, curled up with a gift from her—his first stuffed animal, a plump dog he had named Theophrastus.

Ted celebrated his birthdays with noisy parties of dozens of neighborhood children wearing funny costumes and hats.

In the winter he built tunnels in the snow in the backyard and went sledding and ice-skating in Forest Park.

When spring arrived, he marched his toy soldiers around on the front porch, with his three-legged bulldog, Rex, for company.

He and his best friend, Bill, would roam the neighborhood. Neighbors were always interesting to him: a family named the Bumps, a dentist who treated patients in his own home, two women who didn't mind when Ted practiced his bugle (they were hard-of-hearing), the nosy man across the street (he ran the local paper, the *Springfield Union*).

Ted and Bill and the other Fairfield Street boys invented ways to test each other—like chin-up or ear-wiggling contests. All year round they explored Forest Park, with its lily ponds, trout streams, bike paths, and tennis courts.

During summers at a beach cottage, Ted went fishing with his father, built sand castles, learned to swim, dug in the sand for clams. The family sang or told stories at night, usually outside, where Ted could count fireflies and stars.

Parades around Springfield were happy days. There was so much to take in—circus acrobats, flashy marching bands with trumpets blasting and drums pulsing, people twirling by on bicycles of all kinds.

Ted did begin noticing ways he didn't really fit in around Springfield. He spoke German as well as English. His grandparents were German immigrants, and the Geisels were always the outsiders compared with families that had lived there for generations.

Events in Europe were causing anger at German Americans here. Thoughtless children at school teased Ted for having a German name, singing German songs, eating German food, and whatever else they could think of—even having a dog with three legs.

Sometimes they chased him or beat him up. It was on the playground that Ted developed his strong awareness of injustice.

On top of all that, the Geisel family business was a brewery. Plenty of Springfield citizens frowned on people who drank beer.

Nor did Ted always fit in at home. Both his parents were skilled at rifle shooting and won trophies for it. Every morning his father practiced shooting holes in paper targets for half an hour. He was always urging Ted to take up target shooting or some competitive sport.

But Ted was bored by shooting, and he avoided athletics whenever he could. Gym teachers sighed at his lack of muscles.

Certainly, no one he knew seemed to like drawing as much as he did. Sometimes he even drew on his bedroom walls with his crayons. Everyone was horrified, except for his mother.

He drew the animals he saw in his father's zoo, he drew imaginary creatures, he drew whatever popped into his head.

Like his friends, he adored *Krazy Kat* and other comic strips. Ted would run up to the corner each night to greet his father—then grab the comics page from his father's newspaper.

One day, when Ted was twelve and was doodling as usual, he found himself sketching a funny little cartoon of a man reeling in a giant fish. His parents helped him enter the drawing in a contest run by the *Springfield Union*.

Ted won first prize!

But when he tried taking an art class in high school (the only one he ever took), his teacher scolded him for breaking rules. She thought he was fooling around. The day she warned him he would never be successful at art, he quit the class.

Ted did break rules. He was starting to notice when rules didn't make sense. And he already knew his art broke the rules. His biggest "crime" was exaggerating things. The creatures he drew had ears nine feet long. His horses had wings. His cows could fly as well. His animals looked like plants. His plants looked like animals.

He just had this unusual way of looking at the world, and more often than not, this seemed like a bad thing to other people.

Ted turned thirteen in 1917, the year that the United States declared war on Germany and entered World War I. Luckily, no one could question his patriotism. He was a proud Boy Scout selling United States Liberty Bonds to support the war effort. Walking door to door around Springfield, he collected so much money that he became one of the top ten bond-selling Scouts in town. Now he was going to receive an award.

Ted stood on a platform in front of city hall, grinning at his family and the thousands of Springfieldians who turned out that sunny morning. Ex-president Theodore Roosevelt stirred up the crowd with a speech, then walked down the line of Scouts, handing out medals and congratulating each one.

Ted stood up straight. But when the former president came to him, Roosevelt blurted, "What's this little boy doing here?"

It seemed Roosevelt had only nine medals, and Ted was the tenth Scout in line. No one knew what to do. After a painful silence, Ted was guided offstage.

His usual instinct was to be awkward in public, and after that day he tried to avoid being in public at all.

Ted's parents soon learned he was never going to be studious like his sister, Marnie. In class he doodled instead of taking notes. Sometimes he skipped class altogether, to go to the movies.

Even his mother frowned at him then, warning that people who went to movies in the daytime ended up as failures, not doctors.

In high school he played the banjo, wrote stories and drew cartoons for the school paper, and got classmates to laugh. They voted him "Class Artist and Class Wit."

Ted did have one teacher who encouraged him—his favorite English teacher. He urged Ted to apply to his old school, Dartmouth College, in nearby New Hampshire.

Many around Springfield were astonished when Ted did make it to Dartmouth, fulfilling his mother's dream.

In college everyone also admired his talent for silliness. He was clearly gifted, though no one knew at exactly what. It wasn't as if men could doodle for a living.

His best times were writing verse and drawing for the *Jack-O-Lantern,* the college humor magazine. But after one too many parties with his fraternity brothers, the college forced him to resign as the *Jack-O-Lantern*'s editor.

Ted got around this punishment by writing for the magazine under another name. Partly for his own amusement, he had been experimenting with signing different names to his work. It was at Dartmouth that he started using "Seuss"—his mother's maiden name and his own middle name.

Classmates, on their way to becoming doctors and lawyers and bankers, voted Ted Geisel "Least Likely to Succeed."

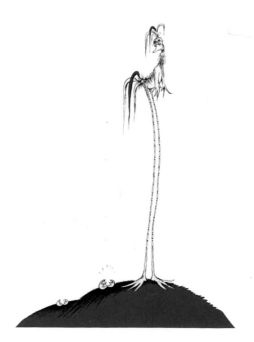

After college he was plagued with more doubts than ever. He had no money, no job prospects. He did have a place to go—he could always move back into his parents' house in Springfield. But wouldn't this be a step backward? Was he forever to be the boy on Fairfield Street?

Stalling for time, he applied for a prestigious grant to study English literature at Oxford University in England and led his parents to believe he was getting it. Unfortunately, someone else got the grant. But Ted's father had already bragged to the editor at the *Springfield Union*—which published the big news. To save face, Ted's father came up with the money to send his son the exaggerator to Oxford anyway.

Now Ted was supposed to be doing serious work, studying early Anglo-Saxon poetry and the plays of William Shakespeare. Instead, he was off doodling and scrawling little poems, as usual.

Then one day a classmate he had a crush on looked over his shoulder. She whispered for his ears alone, "That's a very good flying cow."

Oddly enough, this one remark suddenly put the world into focus for Ted. This was him—a guy who loved to draw animals and loved to write verse.

With more encouragement from his classmate, Ted decided to leave school.

He moved back to Fairfield Street for the time being. All of his energy would now go into finding ways to make money doing what he loved, not what others might want him to do.

Ted began flooding the mailrooms of New York magazines and newspapers with funny articles and animal drawings. Hundreds of them—an entire zoo of crazy birds and beasts.

Then one morning in July, the postman rang the bell at 74 Fairfield Street with an acceptance letter. *The Saturday Evening Post,* a major magazine, offered him $25 for a cartoon of two American tourists riding camels.

Ted let out a hoot and ran upstairs to tell his parents—with a little exaggeration—that the *Post* was going to publish all his drawings from now on.

Instead, other magazines started wanting his drawings of creatures—and it all began to seem like a dream.

Ted's response? He sent out more drawings than ever, fantastical beasts, imaginary settings. He took to signing his latest work "Dr. Theophrastus Seuss" or just "Dr. Seuss." The name tickled him—it had that "doctor" ring to it that he and his family liked so much. Plus, then he could save "Ted Geisel," his real name, for the Great Works that he would dash off in some vague future.

At first, people around the country who saw these new cartoons by Dr. Seuss wrote letters of complaint. A prisoner on death row wrote to say he didn't mind dying if Ted's work was the best publishers could do.

But he also got fan mail. Some people seemed to really appreciate his work. In fact, one day he even received a request for his autograph from a twelve-year-old boy.

Ted glowed for days. This letter pleased him no end. Not so much the autograph part. It was that a young person had asked for it.

Was it possible that his work could be good for children? The boys and girls now growing up on Fairfield Street? Now, *that* sounded interesting. It meant he could share his own love of reading, animals, and justice.

He could even promote fooling around.

By the time August arrived, Ted was packing his suitcases. It was time to say farewell to his parents and take a train to the big city—New York—to find his own place to live.

He found it—a tiny apartment in Greenwich Village—and that Monday, Ted Geisel got busy at his old wooden drawing board. He had his colored pencils, his paints, his typewriter, many erasers, and his furry stuffed dog, Theophrastus. He had all day to work, and all night if he needed it. He was prepared to work hard.

He was twenty-two years old, and his future looked bright.

ON BEYOND FAIRFIELD STREET

Theodor Seuss Geisel was born on March 2, 1904, in Springfield, Massachusetts, and spent his childhood there.

At twenty-two he moved to a studio apartment in New York City, the center of the publishing world. He soon found steady work as a staff writer and artist for *Judge*—"the world's wittiest weekly," as it called itself.

To celebrate, he went out for a spaghetti dinner with the woman who had told him, "That's a very good flying cow." Her name was Helen Palmer. Ted married her when he was twenty-three, and she never stopped encouraging him.

Ted moved on to advertising, drawing bizarre bugs for Flit, a popular insect repellent. This work left him with a lot of money and free time and more energy than ever. He wrote an alphabet book starring his weird animals. Every publisher rejected it.

A few years later, while coming back from Europe on a ship, Ted was distracted by the rhythm of the ship's engines. The rhythmical phrase "And to think that I saw it on Mulberry Street" popped into his head. He remembered the street name from Springfield, and he used it to create a children's story that was rejected by twenty-seven publishers. The twenty-eighth, where an old Dartmouth classmate worked, published it in 1937. Ted was thirty-three.

Back in Springfield, neighbors worried that this new book, *And to Think That I Saw It on Mulberry Street* by "Doctor" Seuss, was some kind of nosy account of real people and their medical problems. But Ted had taken his memories of parades around Springfield and constructed a fantasy about a boy whose imagination is too wild for adults.

The book made little money, but the reviews were fantastic.

Ted kept up his advertising work and continued trying out children's book ideas. One morning he noticed a stranger wearing a pompous hat on the train from Springfield to New York. He began thinking up a story that involved forty-eight hats, adding more and more until he had *The 500 Hats of Bartholomew Cubbins.*

Another morning a breeze blew the sketches around on his drawing board, and an elephant suddenly appeared to be sitting in a tree. This was the birth of *Horton Hatches the Egg.*

During World War II, Ted joined the Army and was sent to Hollywood, where he wrote documentaries for the military.

His first postwar book was *McElligot's Pool,* which he dedicated to his father the fisherman. It remains many people's favorite Dr. Seuss book and was the first to win a Caldecott Honor citation from the American Library Association. Another Caldecott Honor Book followed, *Bartholomew and the Oobleck,* and then a third, *If I Ran the Zoo,*

which came out of his experiences at the Forest Park Zoo.

Reviewers raved that Dr. Seuss books were not like any others previously published for children. They were incredibly funny, with a momentum that propelled readers to the end. They were always respectful toward children, and not always respectful toward authority—the rule makers.

By 1948, Ted and Helen had moved to a large house in La Jolla, California. Ted's studio overlooked the Pacific Ocean, but he usually kept his desk turned away from the view.

Surrounded by doodles, with Theophrastus always near his drawing board, he worked every day of the week, starting each morning at around nine o'clock. Draft after draft, sketch after sketch—the creative process boiled down to two things, he believed, "time and sweat." Sometimes he wasn't satisfied with his work until midnight.

He wrote and drew to please himself. He was happy when the results pleased others, though he occasionally felt a little awkward about being known only as a children's book writer. As the years went by, his "Great Works" for adults didn't happen.

The year 1957 was Ted's electric year. One day his publisher gave him a challenge—to write a story using a list of the words first graders needed to learn to read. With just 225 of the words, he wrote *The Cat in the Hat.* The book did not come to him in a flash—it took him a year to write—but it went on to instant success. At age fifty-three, he would never have to worry about money again.

That same year *How the Grinch Stole Christmas!* appeared—another book over which he sweated but that became an instant classic.

Three years later, his publisher bet Ted $50 that he couldn't write an entire book using only fifty words. The result was *Green Eggs and Ham,* for many years his most popular book. Millions of children all over the world made the switch from "not a reader" to "I can read" while reciting the tale of Sam-I-am. Dr. Seuss became a beloved icon.

But Ted Geisel wasn't *born* Dr. Seuss. Instead, the birth of "Dr. Seuss" was a long process, not all of it comfortable, of searching for a focus.

After he started Beginner Books with *The Cat in the Hat,* he invented another name—Theo. LeSieg (Geisel spelled backward)—that he used for some books he wrote but did not illustrate.

Helen died in 1967, and Ted married Audrey Stone Dimond. As he grew older, his books became more openly serious. He called *The Lorax,* which came out of his anger at pollution, his favorite. It was published in 1971 but took ten years to become as popular as his other books.

In 1974, a newspaper published a piece called "Richard M. Nixon, Will You Please Go Now!" It was a parody of Ted's book *Marvin K. Mooney Will You Please Go Now!,* used with his permission. Nine days later, President Nixon, embroiled in the Watergate scandal, resigned.

In 1984 came *The Butter Battle Book,* Ted's creative response to the race for nuclear arms. He started calling this his best book.

You're Only Old Once!, which is about old age, was published on his eighty-second birthday. That year he returned to Springfield, strolling down Mulberry Street, visiting the owners of his old house on Fairfield Street. Hundreds of children gathered to chant, "We love you, Dr. Seuss!" Stage fright had remained a problem for him, and he avoided the spotlight whenever possible. But on this day he walked through the crowd, shaking hands, and could be seen wiping away tears.

In 1990, his fastest-selling book, *Oh, the Places You'll Go!,* was published. It contained echoes of many of his previous books.

He had been awarded a special Pulitzer Prize, plus honorary doctorates from seven universities (including Dartmouth, his alma mater). His books sold hundreds of millions of copies—the bestselling children's books ever. He often credited life on Fairfield Street for all he had accomplished.

He gave money away to libraries, art museums, scholarship funds, charities, and, of course, zoos.

On September 24, 1991, when he died at age eighty-seven, many people felt as if they'd lost a close personal friend.

In Springfield today, you can visit the Dr. Seuss National Memorial Sculpture Garden. And wherever you live, you can read his books—all still in print.

GREAT WORKS WRITTEN AND ILLUSTRATED BY DR. SEUSS

And to Think That I Saw It on Mulberry Street, 1937

The 500 Hats of Bartholomew Cubbins, 1938

The King's Stilts, 1939

The Seven Lady Godivas, 1939

(not a children's book and now out of print)

Horton Hatches the Egg, 1940

McElligot's Pool, 1947

Thidwick the Big-Hearted Moose, 1948

Bartholomew and the Oobleck, 1949

If I Ran the Zoo, 1950

Scrambled Eggs Super!, 1953

Horton Hears a Who!, 1954

On Beyond Zebra!, 1955

If I Ran the Circus, 1956

How the Grinch Stole Christmas!, 1957

The Cat in the Hat, 1957

The Cat in the Hat Comes Back, 1958

Yertle the Turtle and Other Stories, 1958

Happy Birthday to You!, 1959

Green Eggs and Ham, 1960

One Fish Two Fish Red Fish Blue Fish, 1960

The Sneetches and Other Stories, 1961

Dr. Seuss's Sleep Book, 1962

Hop on Pop, 1962

Dr. Seuss's ABC, 1963

Fox in Socks, 1965

I Had Trouble in Getting to Solla Sollew, 1965

The Cat in the Hat Songbook, 1967

The Foot Book, 1968

I Can Lick 30 Tigers Today! and Other Stories, 1969

I Can Draw It Myself, 1970

Mr. Brown Can Moo! Can You?, 1970

The Lorax, 1971

Marvin K. Mooney Will You Please Go Now!, 1972

The Shape of Me and Other Stuff, 1973

Did I Ever Tell You How Lucky You Are?, 1973

There's a Wocket in My Pocket!, 1974

Oh, the Thinks You Can Think!, 1975

The Cat's Quizzer, 1976

I Can Read with My Eyes Shut!, 1978

Oh Say Can You Say?, 1979

Hunches in Bunches, 1982

The Butter Battle Book, 1984

You're Only Old Once!, 1986

Oh, the Places You'll Go!, 1990

FOR FURTHER READING

Cott, Jonathan. *Pipers at the Gates of Dawn: The Wisdom of Children's Literature.* New York: Random House, 1983.

Morgan, Judith, and Neil Morgan. *Dr. Seuss and Mr. Geisel: A Biography.* New York: Random House, 1995.

Weidt, Maryann N. *Oh, the Places He Went: A Story About Dr. Seuss.* Minneapolis: Carolrhoda Books, 1994.

eSeuss: www.eseuss.com

Forest Park: www.springfieldparks.com/parks/forestpark.htm

Random House's Seussville: www.seussville.com

Springfield History: www.quadrangle.org/springfield-history.htm

The Zoo in Forest Park: www.forestparkzoo.com

www.seussentennial.com

To Andy Krull, for reading me *Green Eggs and Ham*—and all my nieces and nephews.
—K.K.

To Janet—for inviting us to share in the life of Ted Geisel.
—S.J. & L.F.

www.seussentennial.com

Library of Congress Cataloging-in-Publication Data
Krull, Kathleen.
The boy on Fairfield Street : how Ted Geisel grew up to become Dr. Seuss / by Kathleen Krull ; illustrated by Steve Johnson & Lou Fancher. — 1st ed.
    p.   cm.
SUMMARY: Introduces the life of renowned children's book author and illustrator Ted Geisel, popularly known as Dr. Seuss, focusing on his childhood and youth in Springfield, Massachusetts.
ISBN 0-375-82298-4 (trade) — ISBN 0-375-92298-9 (lib. bdg.)
1. Seuss, Dr.—Childhood and youth—Juvenile literature.
2. Authors, American—20th century—Biography—Juvenile literature.
3. Illustrators—United States—Biography—Juvenile literature.
4. Children's literature—Authorship—Juvenile literature.
[1. Seuss, Dr.—Childhood and youth.   2. Authors, American.   3. Illustrators.   4. Authorship.]
I. Johnson, Steve, 1960– ill.   II. Fancher, Lou, ill.   III. Title.
PS3513.E2 Z74 2004   813'.52—dc21   2003001754

Book design by Lou Fancher

The Dr. Seuss books from which illustrations used in *The Boy on Fairfield Street* are taken are listed below in the order in which they appear.

Endpapers (from left to right):
Oh, the Thinks You Can Think!
The Sneetches and Other Stories
Green Eggs and Ham
The Cat in the Hat
Fox in Socks
Dr. Seuss's ABC
There's a Wocket in My Pocket!
How the Grinch Stole Christmas!
One Fish Two Fish Red Fish Blue Fish
Yertle the Turtle and Other Stories
There's a Wocket in My Pocket!
The Cat in the Hat
Scrambled Eggs Super!
Page 7: *And to Think That I Saw It on Mulberry Street*
Page 8: *If I Ran the Zoo*
Page 10: *Green Eggs and Ham*
Page 12: *One Fish Two Fish Red Fish Blue Fish*
Page 14: *The Foot Book*
Page 16: *The Sneetches and Other Stories*
Page 18: *Fox in Socks*
Page 20: *One Fish Two Fish Red Fish Blue Fish*
Page 22: *The Butter Battle Book*
Page 24: *Fox in Socks*
Page 26: *Scrambled Eggs Super!*
Page 28: *The Sneetches and Other Stories*
Page 30: *The 500 Hats of Bartholomew Cubbins*
Page 32: *The Cat in the Hat*
Page 34: *Oh, the Thinks You Can Think!*
Page 36: *Oh, the Places You'll Go!*
Page 38 (from top to bottom):
Fox in Socks
Green Eggs and Ham
And to Think That I Saw It on Mulberry Street
The 500 Hats of Bartholomew Cubbins
Page 39 (from top to bottom):
Horton Hatches the Egg
If I Ran the Zoo
Bartholomew and the Oobleck
Oh, the Places You'll Go!
Dr. Seuss's Sleep Book
One Fish Two Fish Red Fish Blue Fish
Page 40 (from top to bottom):
The Cat in the Hat
How the Grinch Stole Christmas!
Green Eggs and Ham
The Lorax
The Butter Battle Book
Page 41 (from top to bottom):
You're Only Old Once!
One Fish Two Fish Red Fish Blue Fish
Oh, the Places You'll Go!
Yertle the Turtle and Other Stories
Page 42 (from top to bottom):
One Fish Two Fish Red Fish Blue Fish
The Cat in the Hat
One Fish Two Fish Red Fish Blue Fish
Page 43 (from top to bottom):
There's a Wocket in My Pocket!
Oh, the Places You'll Go!
Scrambled Eggs Super!